# STEPHEN STILLS

# BIOGRAPHY

The Soundtrack of the '60s and '70s –

The Stories Behind the Songs

**TOM M. TRAINER**

Stephen stills

Disclaimer

This book contains information that is solely meant to be educational. Despite their best efforts to present accurate and current information, the author and publisher disclaim all expressed and implied representations and warranties regarding the availability, completeness, accuracy, reliability, suitability, or suitability of the content contained herein for any purpose. The publisher and the author disclaim all responsibility for any loss or harm, including without limitation, consequential or indirect loss or damage, or any loss or damage at all resulting from lost profits or data resulting from using this book.

Stephen stills

# TABLE OF CONTENTS

Stephen stills

# INTRODUCTION

Music is more than just sound; it's a reflection of the world around us, a time capsule of emotions, ideas, and cultural shifts. Few musicians embodied this better than **Stephen Stills**. His songs were not just melodies and lyrics; they were statements, personal stories, and moments of history wrapped in chords and harmonies.

If you were alive in the 1960s and 1970s, Stephen Stills' music was impossible to ignore. If you weren't, you've still felt its impact. His songwriting and guitar playing shaped some of the most iconic moments in rock history, whether through **Buffalo Springfield**, **Crosby, Stills & Nash (and Young)**, **Manassas**, or his solo work. His songs captured the spirit of a generation—whether it was the unrest of the Vietnam War, the search for love and identity, or the struggles of personal growth.

Stills wasn't just a performer; he was a **storyteller**. Each song he wrote had a purpose, a message, or a personal truth buried within its lyrics. "For What It's Worth" became the **anthem of protest** in the late 1960s, even though it was originally written about clashes between police and young people on the Sunset Strip. "Suite: Judy Blue Eyes" was an **open love letter** to his former girlfriend, folk singer Judy Collins, and its intricate structure made it one of the most beloved folk-rock songs ever. "Love the One You're With" took on a life of its own as a **celebration of the free love era**, though Stills always insisted it wasn't meant to be taken so literally.

But beyond the hits, there are **hidden gems**—songs that reveal the deeper layers of his talent, his pain, his humor, and his vision. His work with **Manassas**, an ambitious fusion of rock, folk, blues, country, and Latin music, proved he was never content to stay in one lane. His collaborations with legends like **Jimi Hendrix, Eric Clapton, and Bill Withers** showed the respect he commanded among his peers.

This book is a journey through the music of Stephen Stills, focusing on the stories behind the songs. What inspired them? What was happening in his life and in the world at the time? How did they come to be recorded? Through a mix of history, personal anecdotes, and musical analysis, we'll dive into the tracks that made him one of the most influential artists of his era.

Stephen Stills once said, **"The thing I love about music is that it makes people feel something."** This book is dedicated to that feeling—the emotions his music stirred in millions of listeners and the stories behind the songs that became the soundtrack of the '60s and '70s.

Let's explore the legacy of a man who didn't just **play** music—he **lived** it.

# CHAPTER 1: EARLY DAYS AND INSPIRATIONS – CHILDHOOD AND MUSICAL BEGINNINGS

Stephen Arthur Stills was born on January 3, 1945, in Dallas, Texas. Though he would later become one of the most influential musicians of his time, his early life was anything but settled. His father was a military man, which meant the family moved frequently. This transient lifestyle exposed Stills to different cultures, musical styles, and experiences that would later influence his songwriting and playing.

From a young age, Stills was drawn to music. His first exposure to rhythm and melody came from the folk and country sounds of the American South. His family lived in various states, including Florida and Louisiana, where blues and Cajun music were part of everyday life. Even as a child, Stills was fascinated by the way music could convey emotions. He would listen intently to records, picking up the nuances of different instruments and vocal harmonies.

During his teenage years, Stills developed a strong appreciation for the guitar. Unlike some musicians who are classically trained, his approach was largely self-taught. He had a natural ear for music and would spend hours practicing chords, picking styles, and mimicking the sounds he heard on the radio. By the time he reached high school, he was already playing in local bands.

Stills attended **Lincoln High School in Gainesville, Florida**, where he further honed his musical skills. He was never particularly drawn to academics, but when it came to music, he was deeply committed. He spent more time learning songs and playing with friends than he did focusing on schoolwork. His interest in folk music grew during these years, as he was drawn to the storytelling aspect of the genre. He admired artists like Woody Guthrie, Pete Seeger, and The Weavers, who used music as a tool for expression and social commentary.

One of the most pivotal moments in Stills' early years was discovering the power of **harmony singing**. Unlike many aspiring guitarists who focused solely on riffs and solos, Stills became obsessed with how voices could blend together to create something larger than the sum of their parts. This would later become a defining feature of his work with Crosby, Stills & Nash.

Another major influence was **Latin music**. His family spent time in Central America, particularly in Costa Rica and Panama, where he absorbed the rhythmic complexity of Latin sounds. He was intrigued by the way percussion and guitar interacted in Latin music, a style he would later incorporate into his own compositions. This exposure gave him a broader musical palette compared to many of his contemporaries, who were primarily influenced by American and British rock and folk.

After high school, Stills briefly attended **the University of Florida**, but it didn't take long for him to realize that college wasn't for him. Music was his true passion, and he was determined to make it his career. He dropped out and moved to

New York City, where the burgeoning **Greenwich Village folk scene** was in full swing. This was the early 1960s, a time when folk artists like Bob Dylan, Joan Baez, and Phil Ochs were redefining popular music.

Stills played in various folk groups, including **The Continentals**, but he was still searching for his own voice. He knew he had the talent, but he hadn't yet found the right combination of musicians to bring his ideas to life. That moment would come when he made his way to California—a move that would change his life forever.

Folk Roots and Blues Influence

By the time Stephen Stills reached his late teens, he had developed a deep passion for **folk and blues music**, two genres that would heavily shape his songwriting and guitar playing. Unlike many musicians who focused solely on rock and roll, Stills was drawn to the **storytelling** and **emotional depth** that folk and blues offered. He admired the way these genres could capture personal struggles, social injustices, and cultural history in a way that felt both timeless and immediate.

Discovering Folk Music

Stills' first exposure to folk music came through the records his parents owned and the music he heard on the radio. Artists like **Woody Guthrie, Pete Seeger, Lead Belly, and The Weavers** played a major role in shaping his early understanding of the power of song. These musicians weren't just performers; they were storytellers, using their lyrics to comment on the struggles of working-class people, civil rights, and political upheaval.

As Stills moved into his teenage years, he discovered the **Greenwich Village folk scene**, which was thriving in New York City in the early 1960s. Though he hadn't yet moved there himself, he became deeply interested in what was happening in that musical movement. Folk music had become the **voice of activism**, with artists like **Bob Dylan, Joan Baez, Phil Ochs, and Peter, Paul and Mary** leading the charge. Stills was captivated by the simplicity yet profound impact of folk songs—just a voice, a guitar, and a message could change the way people thought about the world.

Stills wasn't just a passive listener; he actively studied the way folk musicians played guitar. He admired the **fingerpicking techniques** of players like Mississippi John Hurt and Doc Watson. These intricate picking styles allowed for a richer, more melodic approach to guitar playing, something Stills would incorporate into his own music later on.

Blues: The Soul of Stills' Sound

While folk music provided Stills with lyrical inspiration, **the blues gave him his soul**. From a young age, he was drawn to the raw emotion of blues music, particularly the work of artists like **Robert Johnson, Muddy Waters, Howlin' Wolf, and B.B. King**. Unlike folk, which was often politically charged and poetic, blues was **personal**, dealing with themes of love, loss, hardship, and perseverance.

Stills was especially fascinated by the **bending techniques and open tunings** used in blues guitar. These elements gave the music a deep, expressive quality that felt almost like human speech. He spent countless hours perfecting his blues technique, experimenting with **slide guitar**, **bent notes**, and **call-and-response phrasing**, which would later become key features of his distinctive guitar style.

Blues wasn't just about technique—it was about **feel**. Stills admired the way blues musicians could express pain and joy through a single note. It wasn't about playing fast or complex; it was about **playing with emotion**. This understanding of the blues would later influence his solo work, as well as his contributions to Buffalo Springfield and Crosby, Stills & Nash.

Merging Folk and Blues into His Own Style

What made Stephen Stills unique was his ability to **blend folk and blues into a cohesive sound**. Many musicians of the time stuck to one genre or the other, but Stills saw no reason why they couldn't coexist. He wanted the lyrical depth and storytelling of folk combined with the raw, expressive power of blues guitar.

When Stills played in coffeehouses and folk clubs in the early 1960s, he stood out. His guitar playing was more **dynamic and aggressive** than many of the folk musicians around him. He wasn't content to just strum chords—he wanted to explore intricate picking patterns, blues-infused solos, and unexpected chord changes. This approach would become a hallmark of his later work, particularly in songs like **"Bluebird"** (Buffalo Springfield) and **"Black Queen"** (his solo album).

The Move to New York and the Folk Scene

In the early 1960s, Stills made his way to **New York City**, where the folk revival was in full swing. He performed in clubs and small venues, meeting other aspiring musicians and soaking in the energy of the scene. He played in a group called **The Continentals**, and though it was a stepping stone, he knew he was meant for something bigger.

It was during this period that Stills refined his **songwriting skills**. He learned that a song didn't need to be overly complicated to be powerful. Sometimes, a few well-chosen words and a simple melody could make a lasting impact. He also realized that his voice—though not as smooth or polished as some singers—had a unique **grit and character** that made his songs feel authentic.

Stills' time in New York was a crucial period of growth, but he felt something was missing. He wanted to move beyond the **confines of folk music** and experiment with **electric sounds**. He dreamed of forming a band that could bridge the gap between folk, blues, and rock. That dream would soon become a reality when he made his way to **California**, where he would meet a young Canadian musician who shared his vision: **Neil Young**.

## Meeting Neil Young and Forming Buffalo Springfield

By the mid-1960s, Stephen Stills had gained experience playing in folk groups and small venues, but he was still searching for something bigger. His time in New York had helped him refine his songwriting and performance skills, but the folk scene was starting to feel **limiting**. He wanted to **electrify his sound**, blending the storytelling of folk with the raw energy of blues and rock. That vision would start to take shape when he met a young Canadian musician who would become one of his greatest collaborators—and rivals—**Neil Young**.

The First Encounter: Stills and Young Cross Paths

The first time Stephen Stills and Neil Young met, it was almost **by accident**. In the early 1960s, Stills had moved to Los Angeles, where he was trying to break into the music business. He played in various bands and auditioned for different projects, always looking for musicians who shared his passion for blending folk, blues, and rock.

Meanwhile, Neil Young was living in Canada, playing in a band called **The Squires**. Like Stills, Young was deeply influenced by folk and blues but was drawn to the idea of using electric instruments to create something fresh. Stills first heard about Young through **folk singer Richie Furay**, who was also trying to find the right mix of musicians for a new band. Furay had played with Stills in a few projects and was impressed by his guitar skills and songwriting ability.

The **true first meeting** between Stills and Young happened in **Thunder Bay, Ontario, Canada**. Stills was traveling with another band at the time, and he happened to hear Neil Young playing with The Squires. Immediately, Stills was drawn to Young's **guitar tone** and **unique vocal style**. There was something raw and unpredictable about Young's playing, and Stills knew that they could create something exciting together.

However, the meeting was brief, and the two went their separate ways—**for the moment**.

The Fateful Reunion in Los Angeles

By 1966, Stills had settled in **Los Angeles**, hoping to form a band that could take folk-rock to the next level. At the same time, Neil Young and his friend **Bruce Palmer**, a talented bass player, had grown frustrated with the music scene in Canada. They decided to head to **California**, hoping to find greater opportunities.

In one of **rock history's most legendary chance encounters**, Stills and Furay were driving down **Sunset Boulevard** when they saw a **black Pontiac hearse** weaving through traffic. The car belonged to none other than **Neil Young and**

**Bruce Palmer**. Recognizing each other immediately, they pulled over and reconnected.

This moment was **pure fate**—had they not crossed paths that day, Buffalo Springfield might never have existed. Stills, Young, Furay, Palmer, and drummer **Dewey Martin** quickly realized that they had a **musical chemistry** unlike anything they had experienced before. Their influences meshed perfectly: Stills brought his blues and folk sensibilities, Young added his signature electric edge, Furay contributed harmonies and rhythm guitar, Palmer provided a deep, steady groove on bass, and Martin's drumming kept everything tightly woven together.

# CHAPTER 2 :BUFFALO SPRINGFIELD: THE BIRTH OF A NEW SOUND

Naming themselves **Buffalo Springfield** after a steamroller they saw parked on the street, the band quickly became one of the most exciting acts in Los Angeles. They were pioneers of what would later be called **"folk-rock"**, blending acoustic melodies with electric arrangements.

Unlike some bands that take years to develop their sound, Buffalo Springfield had an **instant spark**. Stills and Young, in particular, formed a **competitive yet creative partnership**. Stills was the more polished musician, with a deep understanding of structure, harmony, and technical playing. Young, on the other hand, had a **wild, unpredictable energy**, often breaking the rules of traditional songwriting. This **contrast** would define much of their career together.

Buffalo Springfield quickly gained a reputation for their **tight harmonies, intricate guitar interplay, and socially conscious lyrics**. They became a house band at the legendary **Whisky a Go Go**, where they honed their live sound and built a devoted following. It wasn't long before they landed a **record deal** and began working on their debut album.

Their first self-titled album, **Buffalo Springfield (1966)**, contained one of the most important protest songs of the 1960s—**"For What It's Worth."**

## "For What It's Worth" – The Anthem of a Movement

Buffalo Springfield had already begun to make a name for themselves in the Los Angeles music scene, but it wasn't until Stephen Stills wrote **"For What It's Worth"** that they truly became a voice of their generation. The song, with its haunting melody and politically charged lyrics, became one of the most recognizable protest anthems of the 1960s, even though it wasn't originally written about the Vietnam War or civil rights—contrary to popular belief.

## The Inspiration Behind the Song

In late 1966, Los Angeles was experiencing a growing **youth rebellion**. The Sunset Strip, known for its clubs and music venues, had become a gathering place for young people, but local authorities and business owners weren't happy about the **crowds and counterculture influence**. The situation escalated when the city imposed a **curfew** to keep young people from gathering in large numbers.

On **November 12, 1966**, a major clash occurred between **young protestors and the police** outside of Pandora's Box, a popular club on the Strip. What started as a peaceful demonstration quickly turned violent, with police using force to break up the crowds. Stills, who had witnessed the unrest firsthand, was deeply affected by what he saw.

Shortly after, he sat down and wrote **"For What It's Worth"**—not as a typical protest song, but as a reflection on the **tensions between youth and authority**. He later described it as a

**"paranoia song,"** capturing the sense of unease that many young people felt at the time.

Recording the Song

Buffalo Springfield recorded **"For What It's Worth"** in December 1966 at Columbia Studios in Hollywood. The song stood out from their usual folk-rock style. Instead of a fast-paced rock song, it had a **slow, eerie groove**, driven by **Stills' haunting guitar riff** and **Dewey Martin's steady, marching drumbeat**.

One of the song's most memorable elements is the **call-and-response between Stills' lead vocals and the harmonized backing vocals** from the rest of the band. This gave the song a sense of urgency, almost like a conversation happening in real time.

Neil Young's subtle, **eerie guitar licks** added another layer to the song, creating a feeling of tension that mirrored the subject matter. Unlike many protest songs of the time, "For What It's Worth" didn't **preach** or **shout**; instead, it **warned**, with an ominous and almost resigned tone.

Lyrics and Meaning

The opening lines are some of the most **iconic lyrics** of the 1960s:

*There's something happening here*
 *What it is ain't exactly clear*

Right away, Stills set the tone—this wasn't a straightforward protest song, but rather a **statement on uncertainty**. Young people could feel that something was shifting in the world, but they weren't always sure what it was or how to respond.

The next lines painted a vivid picture of confrontation:

*There's a man with a gun over there*
*Telling me I got to beware*

This line wasn't about Vietnam or civil rights protests but rather about the **police presence on the Sunset Strip**. However, it resonated far beyond Los Angeles. Across the U.S., young people were facing similar clashes with authority figures, whether in **anti-war demonstrations**, **civil rights marches**, or **student protests**.

The chorus delivered one of the most **chilling warnings in rock history**:

*Stop, children, what's that sound?*
 *Everybody look what's going down*

Rather than calling for direct action, Stills was **urging awareness**. He wasn't telling people what to think—he was telling them to **pay attention**. The song captured the paranoia, fear, and frustration of a generation that felt like the world was on the verge of something big, but they didn't know what.

Cultural Impact and Legacy

"For What It's Worth" was released as a single in **January 1967**, and it quickly **became Buffalo Springfield's biggest hit**. It reached #7 **on the Billboard Hot 100**, introducing the band to a national audience.

However, the song's true power wasn't in its chart success—it was in its **lasting influence**.

Over time, it became a **symbol of the 1960s protest movement**, even though it wasn't originally about Vietnam. **TV networks, documentaries, and films about the era** frequently used the song, reinforcing its association with the political struggles of the time.

During the height of the Vietnam War, **anti-war protestors adopted it as an anthem**, playing it at demonstrations and rallies. Civil rights activists also connected with the song, as it reflected their own battles against oppression and injustice.

The song has since been **covered and sampled** by numerous artists, and its message of awareness and resistance remains relevant today. Whether played in historical retrospectives or modern political protests, **"For What It's**

Worth" continues to be a timeless statement on power, authority, and the need for people to stay vigilant.

Why It Still Matters

Even though the song was written in response to a specific event on the **Sunset Strip**, its themes still **resonate today**. The lyrics speak to **any moment in history** where people feel that something is **changing, uncertain, and possibly dangerous**.

From political movements to protests against social injustice, the song has been used to underscore moments of conflict and transformation. It has appeared in movies, TV shows, and even modern **political campaigns**, proving that its message is **as relevant now as it was in 1967**.

"For What It's Worth" was more than just **Buffalo Springfield's breakthrough song**—it was a **turning point in Stephen Stills' career**. It proved that he had the ability to write songs that **captured the spirit of the times** while also remaining personal and poetic.

Though Buffalo Springfield's time as a band would be **short-lived**, this song cemented their place in history. It also **set the stage for Stills' future work**, showing that he had a unique ability to blend **folk, rock, blues, and political themes** into music that could stand the test of time.

The Rise and Fall of a Legendary Band

Buffalo Springfield may have been short-lived, but their impact on the music world was enormous. The band captured the **spirit of the**

**late 1960s**, blending folk, rock, and country influences into a sound that would help shape the future of rock music. However, despite their success and musical chemistry, **internal conflicts, creative tensions, and external pressures** led to their downfall far sooner than anyone expected.

The Band's Breakthrough

After the release of **"For What It's Worth"**, Buffalo Springfield's popularity skyrocketed. The song's success helped their **self-titled debut album** (1966) gain traction, leading to increased radio play and bigger audiences at their live shows. The band was seen as **one of the most promising acts in the folk-rock movement**, alongside groups like **The Byrds, The Lovin' Spoonful, and Simon & Garfunkel**.

But while "For What It's Worth" became their defining hit, the rest of the album had a **diverse mix of sounds**. Songs like **"Sit Down, I Think I Love You"** (written by Stills) and **"Nowadays Clancy Can't Even Sing"** (written by Neil Young) showcased the contrast between the two primary songwriters.

- **Stills' songs** tended to have a polished, melodic, and structured style.
- **Young's songs** were rawer, more introspective, and unpredictable.

This **duality** was both the band's strength and one of the biggest sources of tension. Stills and Young respected each other's talent but often clashed over **musical direction and leadership**.

Creative Tensions Between Stills and Young

From the very beginning, Stills and Young had **different artistic visions**.

- Stills was known for his **technical expertise, strong leadership, and perfectionism**. He wanted the band to be **tight and well-rehearsed**.
- Young, on the other hand, had a **more spontaneous and experimental** approach to music. He didn't like being told how to play his songs and often preferred to follow his **own instincts**, even if it meant **abandoning structure**.

Their **opposite personalities** led to frequent disagreements. Young would sometimes **refuse to perform his own songs live**, leaving Stills to take the lead in concerts. Stills, frustrated by Young's **unpredictability**, often tried to take control of the band's direction, which only **pushed Young further away**.

These tensions were evident on their second album, **Buffalo Springfield Again (1967)**. While the album featured **some of their best songs**, including **"Bluebird"** (Stills) and **"Mr. Soul"** (Young), the recording sessions were **difficult and fragmented**.

- Young frequently **refused to show up**, leading Stills to take over many of the instrumental parts.
- Stills, feeling the pressure of holding the band together, became increasingly **controlling** in the studio.
- Richie Furay was often caught in the middle, forced to mediate between the two strong-willed musicians.

Despite these challenges, **Buffalo Springfield Again** was a **critical success**, praised for its **innovative sound and strong songwriting**. However, the internal problems were starting to take their toll.

Legal Troubles and Band Fractures

Just as Buffalo Springfield was reaching their peak, **external problems** made things even worse.

- In 1968, Bruce Palmer was **arrested for drug possession and deported to Canada**, forcing the band to replace him with different bass players.
- The band was under constant pressure from their **record label and management**, who wanted them to tour and record at a faster pace.

- The **Los Angeles music scene** was becoming more chaotic, with increasing police crackdowns on the counterculture movement.

Without Palmer's steady bass playing, the group's live performances **became inconsistent**. Tensions between Stills and Young only **escalated**, and Young started **pulling away** from the band even more.

By mid-1968, it became clear that **Buffalo Springfield was falling apart**. Young had grown frustrated with Stills' dominance in the band and decided to **leave** before their third album was even completed.

The Final Album: Last Time Around (1968)

Buffalo Springfield's final album, **Last Time Around**, was more of a **collection of individual**

**songs** than a cohesive band project. By the time it was being recorded, the members were **barely speaking to each other**, and some songs were recorded separately without the full band present.

- **Stills contributed** the emotional ballad **"Four Days Gone"** and the Latin-tinged **"Uno Mundo."**
- **Young provided** one of his most heartfelt songs, **"I Am a Child."**
- **Furay took center stage** on the album's best-known song, **"Kind Woman."**

While the album had **moments of brilliance**, it was clear that **Buffalo Springfield was no longer a functioning band**. Shortly before its release, the group officially **disbanded in May 1968**.

The Breakup: What Went Wrong?

Buffalo Springfield's breakup was the result of **a perfect storm of issues**:

1. **Stills and Young's Rivalry** – Their creative differences were too strong to sustain a long-term partnership.
2. **External Pressures** – Legal troubles, record label demands, and the chaos of the 1960s music industry made it hard for the band to survive.
3. **Lack of Stability** – With Palmer's deportation and lineup changes, they struggled to maintain consistency.
4. **Conflicting Goals** – By 1968, Young wanted to pursue his **own solo career**, while Stills was interested in forming a new band.

Despite their **short time together**, Buffalo Springfield **paved the way** for the **folk-rock and country-rock movements** that followed. Their influence could be heard in bands like **The Eagles, Poco, and America**.

The Aftermath: Where They Went Next

Even though Buffalo Springfield had ended, its members went on to have **legendary careers**:

- **Stephen Stills** quickly teamed up with **David Crosby (The Byrds) and Graham Nash (The Hollies)** to form **Crosby, Stills & Nash (CSN)**—a supergroup that would become one of the most influential bands of the 1970s.
- **Neil Young** launched a **successful solo career**, experimenting with different

styles and becoming one of rock's most unpredictable and respected artists.

- **Richie Furay** formed **Poco**, a band that helped define country rock.

- **Bruce Palmer and Dewey Martin** attempted to keep Buffalo Springfield alive with new members, but the effort was short-lived.

The Legacy of Buffalo Springfield

Despite lasting only **two years**, Buffalo Springfield's impact was **immeasurable**. Their music continues to be **discovered by new generations**, and their songs are still played on classic rock radio stations.

In 1997, the original members reunited briefly when Buffalo Springfield was **inducted into the Rock and Roll Hall of Fame**. While Neil

Young didn't attend, Stills gave an emotional speech, reflecting on their **chaotic yet groundbreaking** time together.

Buffalo Springfield may have been a **band of contradictions—brilliant yet unstable, innovative yet short-lived—but their music remains a lasting symbol of the 1960s.**

Hidden Gems and Deep Cuts

While **"For What It's Worth"** became Buffalo Springfield's defining song and a lasting symbol of the 1960s, the band had a **rich catalog** filled with overlooked gems. Many of these songs showcased **Stephen Stills' songwriting brilliance, guitar skills, and musical experimentation**. Though Buffalo Springfield was short-lived, their albums contained **deep**

**cuts that revealed the band's versatility and the depth of Stills' artistry**.

In this chapter, we'll explore some of Buffalo Springfield's **lesser-known tracks**—songs that may not have been chart-toppers but still **captured the band's spirit and creativity**.

1. "Bluebird" (1967) – Stills' Guitar Masterpiece

From the album **Buffalo Springfield Again**, "Bluebird" is often considered **Stephen Stills' finest moment as a guitarist** during his time with the band. The song is a **showcase of technical mastery, dynamic shifts, and intricate arrangements** that push folk-rock into new territory.

- The **opening acoustic riff** is one of Stills' most **memorable licks**, blending folk picking with bluesy flourishes.

- As the song progresses, it **transitions from folk-rock to full-blown psychedelic rock**, featuring **distorted electric guitar solos** that set it apart from other Buffalo Springfield tracks.
- The **ending is unconventional**, fading out with a **banjo outro**—a sign of Stills' **genre-blending tendencies** that would later be a key part of his work in Crosby, Stills & Nash.

Though "Bluebird" never became a huge radio hit, it was a **favorite among guitar enthusiasts and live audiences**. Many have compared Stills' solo in "Bluebird" to some of the best work by Eric Clapton or Jimi Hendrix.

2. "Hung Upside Down" (1967) – A Soulful and Emotional Stills Composition

Also from **Buffalo Springfield Again**, "Hung Upside Down" is one of **Stephen Stills' most emotional and introspective songs** from his time with the band. It stands out because of its **soulful groove, rich harmonies, and Stills' bluesy vocal delivery**.

Lyrically, the song reflects **feelings of uncertainty and frustration**, which many interpreted as Stills' **reaction to the band's internal struggles**. Lines like:

*Why am I so hung up on myself?*
*Why am I trying to be somebody else?*

suggest an artist who is grappling with **identity and creative control**. Given the **constant battles between Stills and Neil Young,** it's easy to see how this song could have been a personal reflection.

The track also features **horns**, an unusual addition for Buffalo Springfield but a hint of the jazz and R&B influences that Stills would later explore in his solo career.

3. "Go and Say Goodbye" (1966) – Early Country-Rock Experimentation

Released on their debut album, **"Go and Say Goodbye"** is one of the earliest examples of **Buffalo Springfield experimenting with country music**—a genre that would later influence both **Stephen Stills' and Richie Furay's** careers.

- The **twangy, fast-paced rhythm** and **bright vocal harmonies** show how Buffalo Springfield was **blending folk, country, and rock** years before bands like

**The Eagles and Poco** took country rock mainstream.

- Unlike the politically charged "For What It's Worth," this song is a **straightforward breakup song** with a catchy melody and simple, heartfelt lyrics.
- Though it wasn't a major hit, the song was a glimpse of **how Stills was already thinking ahead** and experimenting with sounds beyond traditional folk-rock.

This track is **often overlooked**, but it was a crucial stepping stone in the development of **country-influenced rock music**.

4. "Everydays" (1967) – Jazz Influences and Experimental Arrangements

"Everydays," from **Buffalo Springfield Again,** is one of the most **unusual and experimental**

**songs** Stephen Stills ever wrote during his time with the band. Unlike their folk-rock staples, this song dives into **jazz-influenced chord progressions, free-flowing melodies, and impressionistic lyrics**.

- The **piano-driven intro** and **soft, smoky vocals** give the song a lounge-like atmosphere, making it stand out from the rest of the album.

- Halfway through, the song **explodes into a chaotic, almost avant-garde jazz break**, featuring **distorted guitar licks and wild drumming**—a clear sign that Buffalo Springfield was not afraid to **push musical boundaries**.

- Lyrically, the song is more abstract than Stills' usual storytelling, painting vivid images of **daily life and fleeting moments**.

Though rarely mentioned in discussions of Buffalo Springfield's greatest songs, "Everydays" is a prime example of Stills' **willingness to experiment beyond the folk-rock formula**.

5. "Rock & Roll Woman" (1967) – A Glimpse of CSN's Sound

This track is **one of the earliest examples of the vocal harmonies that would later define Crosby, Stills & Nash**. Released on Buffalo Springfield Again, "Rock & Roll Woman" features:

- **Lush, layered harmonies** that would later become Stills' signature in CSN.

- A **breezy, West Coast feel**, blending folk and rock effortlessly.
- Lyrics that celebrate **independent, free-spirited women**, capturing the **countercultural attitude** of the late '60s.

Many critics see this song as **a direct precursor to the sound Stills would develop with Crosby and Nash**, making it one of the most significant deep cuts in the Buffalo Springfield catalog.

6. "Questions" (1968) – The Song That Became "Carry On"

Originally appearing on Buffalo Springfield's final album, **Last Time Around**, "Questions" is **a short but crucial track** in Stills' songwriting evolution.

If the melody sounds familiar, it's because Stills later **repurposed it into "Carry On,"** the opening track of Crosby, Stills, Nash & Young's **Déjà Vu (1970)**.

- The song features **Stills' signature chord progressions and poetic lyrics**, asking philosophical questions about life and love.
- Though brief, it has **a dreamy, hypnotic quality** that made it the perfect foundation for what would later become one of CSNY's defining songs.
- "Questions" is a great example of how **Stills would take his Buffalo Springfield ideas and refine them for future projects**.

**Why These Songs Matter**

While Buffalo Springfield is often remembered for **"For What It's Worth,"** the band's **hidden**

**gems and deep cuts** showcase **Stephen Stills' full range as a musician**.

- **"Bluebird" and "Hung Upside Down"** highlight his mastery of **guitar-driven rock and blues.**
- **"Go and Say Goodbye"** shows his **early country-rock sensibilities.**
- **"Everydays"** reveals his **love for jazz and experimental arrangements.**
- **"Rock & Roll Woman"** and **"Questions"** give a glimpse of **the future sound of Crosby, Stills & Nash.**

Buffalo Springfield may have been a **short-lived band**, but the music they left behind continues to inspire. Their deep cuts **reward those who dig deeper**, offering a more complete picture of **Stephen Stills' creativity and influence.**

Stephen stills

# CHAPTER 3: THE BIRTH OF CROSBY, STILLS & NASH (AND YOUNG) – A SUPERGROUP IS BORN

By 1968, **Buffalo Springfield was over**, and Stephen Stills was at a crossroads. Despite the success of the band, its internal conflicts, legal troubles, and creative tensions had made it unsustainable. Stills, however, was not about to slow down. If anything, Buffalo Springfield's **dissolution gave him the freedom** to pursue something even bigger—a band that would redefine the sound of folk-rock and push harmonies to a whole new level.

The seeds of **Crosby, Stills & Nash (CSN)** were planted in **Laurel Canyon, California**, the artistic epicenter of the late '60s rock scene. It was a place where musicians lived close to one another, often dropping in unannounced to jam, write songs, or just hang out. Stills, who had become a respected figure in the music community, found himself surrounded by some of the most talented artists of the era.

- **David Crosby**, a former member of **The Byrds**, had been dismissed from his band due to **clashes with bandmates and his increasing radicalism**.
- **Graham Nash**, a member of the British group **The Hollies**, was looking for a fresh start after growing tired of his band's limitations.

Both Crosby and Nash, like Stills, were searching for **a new musical home**—one that allowed for creative freedom, experimentation, and, most importantly, tight three-part harmonies.

The Magic of Three Voices

The moment CSN was truly born happened **at Joni Mitchell's house** in Laurel Canyon. **Stephen Stills and David Crosby were playing a song together when Nash joined in with a high harmony**. The blend of their voices was **instant magic**—something almost otherworldly.

Graham Nash later described it:

*"We sang three-part harmony and we all looked at each other, because we knew we had something special. We knew we had found a sound that nobody else had."*

Unlike Buffalo Springfield or The Byrds, where harmonies were layered over existing arrangements, CSN's harmonies were the **foundation** of their songs. The vocal blend was **as much an instrument as the guitars and drums**.

Stills, known for his **meticulous attention to detail**, became the de facto **musical director** of the group. He was the most experienced instrumentalist, **playing most of the instruments on their debut album**. Crosby brought his **free-spirited creativity**, and Nash provided a **pop sensibility that balanced Stills and Crosby's complexity**.

Building the Sound

While the **harmonies were the heart of CSN**, the band's **instrumental arrangements** were just as important. Stills, already a multi-instrumentalist, took on the role of the group's **lead guitarist, bassist, and even keyboardist in the studio**.

- His **fingerpicking acoustic style**, influenced by blues and folk, became a **trademark sound** of CSN.
- His **love of Latin and jazz rhythms** gave the music **a unique groove** that set them apart from other folk-rock groups.
- He introduced **layered electric guitars**, adding depth to songs that could have otherwise been purely acoustic.

Stills' ability to seamlessly **blend folk, rock, jazz, and blues** created the **distinct sonic identity of CSN**.

---

"Suite: Judy Blue Eyes" – Love and Heartbreak in Song

Every legendary band needs **a signature song,** and for CSN, that song was **"Suite: Judy Blue Eyes."**

Written by **Stephen Stills**, the song was a **deeply personal reflection** on his breakup with singer-songwriter **Judy Collins**. The two had shared a passionate but turbulent relationship, and by the time CSN was forming, they had drifted apart. Stills, heartbroken but inspired, poured his emotions into a **four-part suite that blended folk, rock, and Latin influences**.

Breaking Down the Song

1. **The Opening ("It's getting to the point...")**

- o The song begins with a **gentle yet urgent melody**, setting the tone for the **emotional journey ahead.**
- o Stills' voice carries **a sense of longing and resignation**, reflecting his feelings about the relationship.

2. **The Shift ("What have you got to lose?")**

- o The song takes a **dynamic turn**, becoming more rhythmic and hopeful.
- o The harmonies **soar**, showcasing the **vocal chemistry of CSN.**

3. **The Breakdown ("Chestnut brown canary...")**

- This section brings in **a melancholic beauty**, full of poetic imagery.
- Stills' songwriting reaches its peak here, balancing **personal pain with universal themes.**

4. **The Finale ("Doo doo doo doo doo...")**

- The song **transforms into a Latin-inspired celebration,** complete with **syncopated rhythms and playful melodies.**
- It's a **joyous farewell**, as if Stills is **dancing away his sorrow.**

The Impact

"Suite: Judy Blue Eyes" became the **centerpiece of CSN's self-titled debut album (1969).** It was more than just a song—it was **a statement of artistic ambition**, proving that folk-rock could be as intricate and multi-layered as any other genre.

Stills later admitted that the song was his way of **trying to win Collins back**, but while their romance didn't rekindle, the song remains **one of the greatest love-and-loss ballads ever written**.

The Woodstock Moment

By the time CSN's debut album was released, the group had already built a reputation as one of the **most exciting new acts** in music. But **one performance would cement their place in rock history forever—Woodstock, 1969**.

A Nervous Debut

CSN had only played a handful of live shows before **being booked to play the legendary festival.** When they stepped onto the stage, **they were nervous**—so nervous, in fact, that **Graham Nash introduced the set by saying, "This is only the second time we've played in front of people, man."**

- The band **opened with "Suite: Judy Blue Eyes"**, instantly captivating the massive crowd.
- Their **tight harmonies cut through the night air,** proving that their studio magic was **just as powerful live.**
- Despite the nerves, their **performance was mesmerizing,** and it helped **solidify their place as one of the defining voices of a generation.**

Enter Neil Young

Shortly after Woodstock, **Neil Young joined the group**, transforming CSN into **Crosby, Stills, Nash & Young (CSNY)**. Young's addition brought a **new layer of intensity and unpredictability**, as well as another strong songwriter.

- Young's presence created **a new dynamic**, with **him and Stills reviving their old Buffalo Springfield rivalry**.
- His raw, electric style **contrasted beautifully with CSN's polished harmonies**.
- The band's **follow-up album, Déjà Vu (1970), became even bigger than their debut**, containing classics like **"Teach Your Children" and "Woodstock."**

The Birth of a Legend

The formation of **Crosby, Stills & Nash (and later CSNY)** was **a turning point in rock history**.

- **Stephen Stills** brought the **musicianship and technical expertise**.
- **David Crosby** contributed **his free-spirited creativity**.
- **Graham Nash** added a **sense of melody and structure**.
- **Neil Young** introduced an **edginess and unpredictability**.

Together, they created something **greater than the sum of their parts**.

CSN's **harmonies, storytelling, and genre-blending approach** set the standard for **folk-rock supergroups**. And at the heart of it all was **Stephen Stills—constantly innovating, pushing boundaries, and crafting some of the most memorable songs of the era**.

# CHAPTER 4: PROTEST, POLITICS, AND POWER – "OHIO" – THE TRAGEDY THAT SPARKED A PROTEST SONG

By 1970, Crosby, Stills, Nash & Young had become **more than just a band—they were a voice for a generation**. The Vietnam War was raging, protests were erupting across America, and young people were increasingly **distrustful of their government**. Rock music was no longer just about love and escapism; it was about **speaking truth to power**.

Then, on **May 4, 1970**, something happened that would shake the nation—and inspire **one of the greatest protest songs in history**.

The Kent State Massacre

At **Kent State University in Ohio**, students had gathered to protest **President Nixon's decision to expand the Vietnam War into Cambodia**. What began as peaceful demonstrations quickly escalated, and on that fateful day, the **Ohio National Guard opened fire on unarmed students**.

- **Four students were killed.**
- **Nine others were wounded.**
- **The shootings sent shockwaves across America.**

For many, this was the moment that proved **the government was willing to turn its guns on its own people**.

Neil Young's Immediate Reaction

When **Neil Young** saw photos of the tragedy in a **Life magazine article**, he was **outraged**. He picked up his guitar and, in **a single burst of inspiration**, wrote a song that captured the raw pain and anger of the moment: **"Ohio."**

- The song's opening line—**"Tin soldiers and Nixon coming"**—directly blamed the president for the deaths.
- The chorus—**"Four dead in Ohio"**—was haunting, repeating the tragedy like a chant.
- The song's **urgent, electric guitar riff** made it feel like a call to action.

Young brought the song to the band immediately. **Stills, Crosby, and Nash knew they had to record it—fast.**

A Song That Changed Everything

CSNY rushed to a studio in **Los Angeles** and **recorded "Ohio" in one take**. The urgency of the moment was captured **in the rawness of the performance**—Young's **sharp lead vocals,** Stills' **searing guitar licks**, and the **haunting harmonies** from Crosby and Nash.

- **Within days, "Ohio" was on the radio.**
- **It was banned on some stations** for its anti-Nixon message, but that only made it more powerful.
- **The song became an anthem of resistance**, played at protests and rallies across the country.

Crosby later said:

*"That's the best thing we ever recorded. If you're ever going to get a protest song together, that's the way to do it."*

At a time when music had real political weight, **"Ohio" proved that songs could change minds and inspire action**.

Music as Activism

CSNY had always been political, but "Ohio" cemented them as **one of the most politically engaged bands of their time**. Yet, for **Stephen Stills**, protest music was about more than just making statements—it was about **challenging people to think and act**.

Stills' approach to political songwriting was **different from Neil Young's**. While Young often wrote **direct, explosive protest songs**, Stills had a more **nuanced and introspective** way of tackling social issues.

"Find the Cost of Freedom" – A Reflection on War

Written as the **B-side to "Ohio"**, Stills' song **"Find the Cost of Freedom"** was a chilling, **acoustic lament on the price of war**.

*Find the cost of freedom, buried in the ground. Mother Earth will swallow you, lay your body down.*

Unlike the **rage-fueled energy of "Ohio,"** this song was **quiet and mournful**, showing the personal toll of war. The song's **minimalistic arrangement**—just **vocals and guitar**—made it even more powerful.

It was a reminder that, beyond the headlines and protests, **real people were dying**, both overseas and at home.

"For What It's Worth" – A Protest Song Before Its Time

Though it was written in **1966**, Buffalo Springfield's **"For What It's Worth"** became an **unofficial anthem of the anti-war movement** in the late '60s.

- Originally inspired by the **Sunset Strip riots in Los Angeles,** the song's lyrics were **universal enough to apply to almost any political moment.**
- **"There's something happening here, what it is ain't exactly clear"** captured the unease of a generation.

- The song was **used in Vietnam War protests** and later appeared in countless documentaries about the 1960s.

Stills had written the song before the **Vietnam War protests reached their peak**, proving that he had **a deep understanding of cultural shifts before they fully happened.**

How Stills Balanced Art and Politics

Unlike some artists who **fully immersed themselves in activism, Stephen Stills always walked a fine line between politics and artistry**.

- He never wanted to be **pigeonholed as a protest singer**, preferring to write **about a wide range of human emotions and experiences**.

- While **Neil Young** would sometimes write **blunt, fiery political songs**, Stills preferred to be **more poetic and metaphorical.**
- He saw **music as a unifier**, believing that songs should **make people think rather than divide them.**

Political Tensions Within CSNY

The political nature of CSNY also led to **internal conflicts**.

- Crosby and Young were **the most outspoken activists**, always eager to use the band's platform for political causes.
- Stills, though socially aware, was **more focused on the music itself**.
- This difference in priorities sometimes led to **clashes between Stills and Young,**

especially when it came to song selection for albums.

Despite these tensions, CSNY remained **a band that defined the political spirit of the late '60s and early '70s**.

The Enduring Power of Protest Music

Even decades later, the political songs of **Stephen Stills and CSNY** remain as powerful as ever.

- **"Ohio" is still played at protests and political rallies**.
- **"For What It's Worth" continues to be used in films and documentaries** about civil unrest.
- **Stills' songs remind us that music can both reflect and shape history**.

Stills himself has said:

*"Music has always been a way for people to tell the truth when politicians won't."*

As long as people **fight for justice**, the songs that Stills and his bandmates created will **never lose their power**.

The Legacy of Stills' Political Music

Stephen Stills didn't just **write songs—he wrote history**.

- His work with **Buffalo Springfield** foreshadowed the protests to come.
- His **songs with CSNY gave a voice to a generation** fighting against war and injustice.

- His **ability to balance art and activism** made him one of the most **respected songwriters of his time.**

While **Neil Young may have been the most vocal protester** in the group, **Stills provided the depth and musicianship that made their songs last.** His contributions ensured that CSNY wasn't just a **political band**, but also a **timeless musical force.**

# CHAPTER 5: THE SOLO YEARS – A NEW MUSICAL IDENTITY

After establishing himself as a key force behind **Buffalo Springfield** and **Crosby, Stills, Nash & Young (CSNY), Stephen Stills embarked on a solo career** that allowed him to fully explore his musical identity. Unlike the constraints of a band, where creative decisions had to be shared, **his solo work was entirely his vision**. It was here that he truly demonstrated his versatility, blending **folk, rock, blues, Latin, and jazz** into a sound that was uniquely his own.

During the 1970s, Stills released a series of **critically acclaimed albums**, proving that he was more than just a great bandmate—he was an artist who could stand alone.

Breaking Away: *Stephen Stills (1970)*

In **1970**, Stills released his **self-titled debut solo album**, a record that showcased his full range as a songwriter and musician. The album was **a major commercial success**, peaking at **No. 3 on the Billboard 200** and earning a **gold certification**.

A One-Man Band

Unlike his work with CSNY, where **harmonies and collaboration defined the sound**, *Stephen Stills* was a deeply personal record. Stills took complete control, playing **multiple instruments, handling production duties, and shaping the sound entirely on his own**.

- He played **guitar, bass, keyboards, and percussion**, proving his skills as a **multi-instrumentalist**.
- The album's production was **rich and layered**, combining **rock, blues, folk, and Latin influences**.
- While CSNY's music was often **soft and acoustic**, this album leaned **heavily on electric guitar**, showing a **grittier, more energetic side of Stills**.

A Star-Studded Album

Though Stills played much of the instrumentation himself, he also **brought in some of the biggest names in music** to collaborate:

- **Jimi Hendrix** played **lead guitar on "Old Times Good Times"**, marking **one**

**of his final recorded performances** before his death.

- **Eric Clapton** contributed a blistering **guitar solo on "Go Back Home"**, adding a **British blues-rock influence**.
- **Ringo Starr** (credited as "Richie") played drums on some tracks, bringing his **steady, reliable rhythm**.

The Songs That Defined the Album

1. **"Love the One You're With"**

   - The album's biggest hit, this song became **Stills' signature solo track**.
   - Inspired by **a conversation with Billy Preston**, the song's message—**embrace the love**

around you—resonated deeply in the **free-spirited 1970s**.

- ○ Its **infectious chorus, gospel-style backing vocals, and upbeat rhythm** made it **a classic**.

2. **"Do for the Others"**

- ○ A **gentle acoustic ballad**, showcasing Stills' **introspective side**.
- ○ The lyrics reflected **his feelings of loss and longing**, possibly referencing **his relationships with Judy Collins and Rita Coolidge**.

3. **"Black Queen"**

- ○ A **raw blues song**, featuring **only Stills on acoustic guitar and vocals**.

- His **ferocious guitar playing** and **gritty vocal delivery** made this track stand out as one of his most **passionate solo performances**.

4. **"Sit Yourself Down"**

- A song that combined **rock and gospel**, featuring **uplifting harmonies and an anthemic chorus**.
- This track showed **Stills' ability to blend spirituality with rock music**.

Impact of the Album

*Stephen Stills (1970)* was not just **a successful debut**—it was a **statement**. It proved that **Stills could thrive outside of CSNY**, delivering **hits,**

**experimenting with genres, and collaborating with legends**.

"Love the One You're With" – The Story Behind His Biggest Hit

Of all the songs from his solo career, **"Love the One You're With"** remains **his most iconic**. The song captured the **spirit of the early 1970s**, blending **folk, rock, gospel, and Latin rhythms** into a joyous anthem.

The Inspiration

Stills credited **Billy Preston**—the legendary keyboardist who played with The Beatles—for inspiring the song. During a conversation, Preston told him:

*"If you can't be with the one you love, love the one you're with."*

Stills immediately recognized the **wisdom and universality of the phrase** and set out to write a song around it.

The Music

- The song's **opening acoustic riff** is instantly recognizable.
- The **call-and-response chorus** and **gospel-style backing vocals** give it an uplifting feel.
- Stills' **percussion-heavy rhythm**, influenced by **Latin music**, makes the song **danceable and infectious**.

The Message and Legacy

While some people interpreted the song as a **free-love anthem**, Stills later clarified that it was about **accepting and appreciating the**

**people in your life** rather than longing for something unattainable.

Despite its **deceptively simple lyrics**, the song's **arrangement and performance** made it one of Stills' most **enduring hits**.

- **It reached No. 14 on the Billboard Hot 100.**
- **It became a concert staple for Stills.**
- **It was covered by multiple artists**, including The Isley Brothers and Luther Vandross.

Even today, "Love the One You're With" remains one of the most **instantly recognizable songs of the early '70s**.

Experimentation with Latin and Jazz

One of the things that set **Stills apart from his peers** was his **willingness to experiment with different genres**.

Latin Influence

Having spent part of his youth in **Costa Rica and the Caribbean**, Stills developed a deep love for **Latin music**, which he incorporated into his solo work:

- **Percussion-heavy arrangements**, including **congas and bongos**.
- **Syncopated rhythms**, giving his songs a natural groove.
- **Spanish-style guitar playing**, featuring intricate fingerpicking.

His song **"Cherokee"** (from *Stephen Stills 2*, 1971) is a perfect example of **his Latin**

**influence**, blending **jazz and flamenco-style guitar**.

Jazz Experiments

Stills was also drawn to **jazz**, a genre that allowed for more improvisation and complexity:

- He often used **jazz chord progressions**, giving his music a sophisticated feel.
- He collaborated with **jazz musicians**, including **Herbie Hancock**, who played on some of his later records.

His **fusion of rock, jazz, and Latin music** made his solo albums stand out from the typical **folk-rock sound** of his CSNY peers.

A Solo Artist with Endless Creativity

While Stephen Stills would **always be associated with CSNY**, his solo career showed a **different side of his artistry**.

- His debut album, *Stephen Stills*, proved that he was **a master musician capable of writing timeless hits**.
- His biggest hit, **"Love the One You're With,"** captured the **joy and freedom of the early '70s**.
- His **experiments with Latin and jazz music** set him apart from his contemporaries.

Stills may have shared the stage with some of rock's biggest legends, but as a solo artist, he carved out a **unique identity—one that blended musical mastery with fearless innovation**.

Stephen stills

# CHAPTER 6: MANASSAS – A FUSION OF GENRES

By the early **1970s**, Stephen Stills had already made a name for himself as a **brilliant songwriter, guitarist, and vocalist** through his work with **Buffalo Springfield, Crosby, Stills, Nash & Young (CSNY), and his solo albums**. However, instead of continuing on a purely solo path, he decided to create **something completely new**—a band that could explore his **eclectic musical influences** while giving him the freedom to lead.

This led to the birth of **Manassas**, one of the most musically diverse and underrated bands of the era. Unlike his previous projects, which were often defined by group tensions or industry expectations, Manassas was a place where **Stills**

**could fully experiment with rock, folk, blues, country, Latin, and bluegrass—all in one band**.

Creating a New Sound

The Formation of Manassas

By **1971**, Stephen Stills was searching for a fresh musical direction. He had already released two successful solo albums but wanted a group that could explore **more complex musical arrangements** while still allowing him to maintain control.

Chris Hillman Joins the Project

During this time, **Chris Hillman**, former **bassist and guitarist for The Byrds and The Flying Burrito Brothers**, was looking for a new musical outlet. Hillman had been part of **the**

**early country-rock movement**, and his ability to blend rock with traditional American roots music made him a **perfect match** for Stills.

When **Stills and Hillman crossed paths**, they realized they shared a deep love for many of the same musical styles. This connection led to the idea of forming a **full band**, rather than just another **Stephen Stills solo album**.

The Band Members

Stills and Hillman recruited a group of **exceptionally talented musicians**, each bringing a unique flavor to the sound:

- **Al Perkins (pedal steel guitar, banjo)** – A country and bluegrass specialist, he brought an authentic **Nashville sound** to the group.

- **Joe Lala (percussion)** – His Latin percussion work added a **Caribbean and Afro-Cuban feel** to many of their songs.
- **Paul Harris (keyboards)** – A classically trained pianist, Harris added **jazz and orchestral textures** to the music.
- **Dallas Taylor (drums)** – A longtime Stills collaborator from **CSNY and Stills' solo projects**, he provided the steady rock foundation.
- **Fuzzy Samuels (bass)** – A rhythmic powerhouse, his bass work gave the songs a rich groove.

With this **diverse lineup, Manassas wasn't just a band—it was a musical melting pot**.

---

The *Manassas* Album (1972) – A
Genre-Blending Masterpiece

Manassas' **self-titled debut album**, released in
**April 1972**, was an **ambitious double LP** that
showcased the band's ability to **seamlessly
blend multiple genres**. Each side of the album
had its own **distinct musical identity**, making it
feel like **four mini-albums in one**.

Side 1: The Raven (Rock & Latin)

This section contained **blues-driven rock songs**
with heavy **Latin influences**, demonstrating
**Stills' love for percussive rhythms and
electric guitar solos**.

- **"Song of Love"** – A driving rock song
  that introduced listeners to **Manassas'
  dynamic sound**.

- **"Rock & Roll Crazies/Cuban Bluegrass"** – A perfect example of **genre fusion**, shifting from hard rock to a **bluegrass-infused Latin jam.**

Side 2: The Wilderness (Country & Folk)

Here, Manassas explored **acoustic folk and traditional country sounds**, reflecting **Chris Hillman's influence.**

- **"Fallen Eagle"** – A fast-paced country song criticizing **political corruption.**
- **"Johnny's Garden"** – One of Stills' most **beautiful and personal songs.**

Side 3: Consider (Blues & Ballads)

This section showcased **Stills' blues influences and introspective songwriting.**

- **"It Doesn't Matter"** – A classic Stills ballad with **beautiful harmonies** and a soft rock feel.
- **"Bound to Fall"** – A folk-influenced tune about **life's unpredictability**.

Side 4: Rockin' (Electric Rock & Jams)

The final section of the album brought back **high-energy rock**, closing the record on an **electrifying note**.

- **"The Love Gangster"** – Featuring a **funky groove** and powerful vocals.
- **"Blues Man"** – A heartfelt tribute to **Jimi Hendrix, Duane Allman, and other fallen musical heroes**.

"Johnny's Garden" – A Personal Reflection

One of the **most beloved songs** from the *Manassas* album is **"Johnny's Garden."**

The Inspiration

The song was inspired by **Stills' retreat to the English countryside**. At the time, he owned a home in Surrey, England, which had a **beautiful garden maintained by a caretaker named Johnny**.

- Stills saw **Johnny's garden as a symbol of peace and simplicity**.
- After years of **rock & roll chaos**, he longed for a place of **quiet reflection and escape**.
- The lyrics capture a sense of **nostalgia, longing, and appreciation for life's simple joys**.

## Musical Composition

- The song features **delicate acoustic guitar work** and **soft vocal harmonies**.
- **Hillman's backing vocals** add a **warm, folk-like quality**.
- The melody is **melancholic yet uplifting**, reflecting **Stills' mixed emotions about fame and solitude**.

## Why It's One of Stills' Best Songs

- It showcases **his ability to write deeply personal, poetic lyrics**.
- The song's **gentle arrangement** highlights his **folk and country influences**.
- It remains one of his **most cherished and enduring compositions**, often performed live.

Why Manassas Remains an Underrated Masterpiece

Despite its **brilliance and originality**, *Manassas* never received **the commercial success or mainstream recognition** of Stills' work with CSNY. However, over the years, it has been regarded as one of the **great hidden gems of 1970s rock**.

What Made Manassas Special?

1. **Seamless Genre-Blending** – No other rock band at the time **combined rock, country, folk, blues, and Latin music so effortlessly**.
2. **Virtuoso Musicianship** – Every member of the band was **highly skilled**, creating **a tight, polished sound**.

3. **Lyrical Depth** – Stills wrote **some of his most introspective and poetic lyrics** for this project.

The Band's Short-Lived Run

- After their **critically acclaimed debut**, Manassas released a second album, *Down the Road* (1973), but it **didn't achieve the same level of success**.
- By 1974, **CSNY reunited**, and Stills' focus shifted back to the **supergroup**.
- **Manassas disbanded**, but their music remains a **treasured part of Stills' legacy**.

---

Conclusion: Manassas – A Visionary Musical Experiment

Stephen Stills used **Manassas** as a way to **push musical boundaries** in ways that **Buffalo Springfield and CSNY never could.**

- The band gave him the freedom to explore **new sounds**.
- It allowed him to work with **some of the most talented musicians in rock and country**.
- It produced one of the **most diverse and impressive albums of his career**.

Though **Manassas was short-lived**, its impact remains. For **fans of Stephen Stills**, this band represents one of his **most ambitious and innovative projects**.

# CHAPTER 7: THE CSN (&Y) REUNION YEARS

After the brief but brilliant run of **Manassas**, Stephen Stills found himself drawn back to **Crosby, Stills & Nash (CSN)**, and at times, **Crosby, Stills, Nash & Young (CSNY)**. The chemistry between **David Crosby, Graham Nash, Neil Young, and Stills** was undeniable, and their harmonies, both musical and personal, had left a permanent mark on rock history.

The **mid-1970s to the early 1980s** marked a period of **reunions, breakups, and reinventions** for the group. While tensions remained between the band members—especially between **Stills and Young**—the magic of CSN(&Y) was too strong to ignore.

This chapter explores **how Stills navigated the reunions, the music they created, and the challenges they faced along the way**.

Reuniting with Old Friends

The CSNY 1974 Tour – "The Doom Tour"

By **1974**, **Crosby, Stills, Nash & Young** had been apart for nearly **four years**, each member focusing on **solo projects** or other collaborations. However, they remained one of the **biggest names in rock**, and **promoters were eager for a reunion**.

At the time, **Neil Young was hesitant** but ultimately agreed to **join CSN for a massive stadium tour**. The tour would become legendary—not just for the music, but for the **chaos and excess** that surrounded it.

Key Aspects of the 1974 Tour

- The tour played in **massive stadiums,** marking one of **the first rock "mega-tours" in history**.
- The setlists were **expansive**, featuring **classic CSNY hits**, solo material, and even some **unreleased songs** (some of which later appeared on Young's *Decade*).
- **The band traveled in separate limos and stayed in different hotels**, a sign of the tensions that still lingered between them.
- **Drugs and alcohol were rampant**, leading to **erratic performances**—some nights, they were brilliant; other nights, they fell apart.

Despite the chaos, the tour was **a financial success**, but it failed to **fully rekindle their creative bond**.

The Aftermath

- The tour **was supposed to lead to a new CSNY album**, but **infighting and creative differences** prevented that from happening.
- Young quickly **went back to his solo career**, leaving CSN to continue as a trio.

CSN – The 1977 Comeback Album

Without Young, **Crosby, Stills & Nash** decided to **record a new album as a trio**.

Making the Album

- Unlike their **self-titled 1969 debut**, this album had **a polished, radio-friendly sound**.
- **Stills, Crosby, and Nash all contributed strong material**, but **Stills was the musical backbone**, handling much of the **instrumentation and arrangements**.
- The album became one of their **biggest commercial successes**, showing that **CSN could thrive without Neil Young**.

Key Tracks and Stills' Contributions

1. **"Dark Star"**

   o A **standout track by Stills**, blending **smooth, jazzy guitar licks** with **soulful lyrics about love and loss**.

- ○ Showcased his **signature bluesy guitar work**, reminding fans of his **guitar mastery**.

2. **"See the Changes"**

- ○ A **Stills composition** that had actually been written **during the CSNY era**.
- ○ Lyrically, it reflected on the **passage of time and changing relationships**, themes that were deeply personal for the band.

3. **"Fair Game"**

- ○ A song full of **swagger**, featuring **Latin-inspired rhythms and playful lyrics**.

- o Demonstrated **Stills' continued fascination with world music influences**.

Impact of the Album

- It reached **No. 2 on the Billboard 200** and became one of their best-selling records.
- **Critics praised its harmonies and songwriting**, proving that CSN still had something special together.

However, as always with CSN, **tensions soon resurfaced**, and **the trio struggled to maintain their momentum**.

Navigating the Challenges of Fame

The Late 1970s: More Struggles, More Reunions

The success of the **CSN album (1977)** should have paved the way for more stability, but instead, **the band continued to be plagued by personal struggles**:

- **David Crosby** was battling **severe drug addiction**, which **affected his reliability in the studio and on stage.**
- **Stills and Nash often clashed over musical direction**, with Stills favoring **a harder, bluesier rock sound**, while Nash preferred **more polished, pop-friendly songs**.
- **Neil Young remained unpredictable**, sometimes expressing interest in CSNY projects, then **abandoning them at the last minute.**

CSN 1982 – The Struggles of *Daylight Again*

By **1982**, CSN was facing **serious difficulties**:

- Crosby's **drug problems had worsened**, making it **impossible for him to contribute as much.**
- **The record label pushed for Stills & Nash to continue without Crosby**, leading to **tensions within the group.**
- **Despite the drama, the album produced hits**, including **"Wasted on the Way" (written by Nash) and "Southern Cross" (a Stills classic).**

"Southern Cross" – A Stills Classic

One of Stills' greatest **later-period CSN songs** was **"Southern Cross"**, which became an **instant fan favorite.**

- **Inspired by a sailing trip** he took after a **failed relationship**, the song is a reflection on **love, adventure, and personal growth**.
- Features **rich harmonies, evocative lyrics, and one of Stills' most memorable melodies**.
- Over the years, it has become one of CSN's most **beloved songs**, often played in their live sets.

Despite the **drama behind the album**, *Daylight Again* proved that **CSN could still create hits**, even as they struggled to hold things together.

A Band That Couldn't Stay Apart

Through the **1970s and 1980s**, Stephen Stills found himself **constantly drawn back to CSN** and **CSNY**, despite all the **challenges, fights, and personal struggles**.

- **The chemistry they shared was undeniable**—when they were at their best, their music **defined a generation**.
- **Stills remained the group's musical foundation**, bringing a **rock and blues edge to their sound**.
- Even as **fame, addiction, and ego battles threatened to tear them apart**, they always found their way back to each other.

CSN (&Y) would continue **to reunite in different forms throughout the 1980s, 1990s, and beyond**, but their most **influential and powerful years** had already left an **indelible mark on rock history**.

# CHAPTER 8: STILLS VS. YOUNG – A MUSICAL RIVALRY

Few relationships in rock history have been as **complex, competitive, and compelling** as the one between **Stephen Stills and Neil Young**. From their early days in **Buffalo Springfield** to their battles within **Crosby, Stills, Nash & Young (CSNY)** and their various collaborations and conflicts over the years, their dynamic was marked by **friendship, rivalry, admiration, and frustration**.

This chapter explores the **musical partnership and competition** between Stills and Young—how they **pushed each other to greatness** while **constantly clashing** over artistic direction, leadership, and personal differences.

The Friendship and Competition

Meeting in Canada

The story of **Stills and Young** begins in the early **1960s**, when both were still **unknown musicians** searching for their sound.

- Stills, originally from **Texas and Florida**, had moved to **Los Angeles** to pursue music.
- Young, a **Canadian singer-songwriter**, was performing with his band **The Squires** in Winnipeg.
- Their paths first crossed when **Stills heard Young play** during a visit to Canada.

- Stills was **impressed by Young's raw talent** and distinctive voice but **saw him as a potential rival from the start**.

Though they wouldn't form a band immediately, there was a sense that their **musical paths were destined to collide**.

Buffalo Springfield – A Clash of Visions

Their first real collaboration came when they both ended up in **Los Angeles** in **1966**. Along with **Richie Furay**, they formed **Buffalo Springfield**, a band that blended **folk, rock, and psychedelia**.

From the start, Stills and Young were the **driving creative forces**, but they had **very different styles**:

- **Stills was a natural leader**—ambitious, disciplined, and musically versatile. He had a **strong sense of melody and song structure**.
- **Young was unpredictable**, more interested in **raw emotion and spontaneity than technical precision**.
- Stills wanted **tight arrangements** and well-produced records, while Young preferred **loose, unpolished recordings**.

Their **differences led to frequent conflicts**, with Young often **quitting the band**, only to return later.

For What It's Worth vs. Mr. Soul

One of the most telling moments of their rivalry came when **Buffalo Springfield** scored a massive hit with **"For What It's Worth"**, a song written by **Stills**.

- The song became an **anthem of the 1960s**, cementing **Stills as the group's primary songwriter**.
- Young, always competitive, responded by writing **"Mr. Soul,"** a song that took a **darker, more mysterious approach** to social commentary.
- The contrast between these two songs reflected their **differing artistic visions**—Stills was more **polished and direct**, while Young was more **abstract and edgy**.

Buffalo Springfield eventually **fell apart in 1968**, partly because of **Young's tendency to leave and return unpredictably**. However, the

**Stills-Young rivalry didn't end there**—it only evolved.

"Long May You Run" – The Story of a Broken Partnership

The Stills-Young Band (1976)

Despite their constant competition, Stills and Young respected each other's talent. In **1976**, they decided to collaborate on a full-length album called **Long May You Run**, released under **The Stills-Young Band** name.

- The album was intended to be a **true partnership**, bringing together Stills' **polished musicianship** and Young's **raw energy**.
- However, the project quickly fell apart due to **creative disagreements**.

- **Young abruptly left the tour** before it was finished, leaving Stills **to carry on alone**.

In a **classic Neil Young move**, he left a **handwritten note** for Stills saying:

*"Dear Stephen, funny how some things that start spontaneously end that way. Eat a peach. Neil."*

Stills was **furious**, but Young's exit wasn't a surprise—by this point, their **push-and-pull dynamic was well established**.

The Title Track – A Tribute or a Goodbye?

One of the most enduring songs from the album is **"Long May You Run"**, written by **Young**.

- The song was inspired by **Young's first car**, a **1953 Buick Roadmaster**.

- However, many listeners saw it as **a symbolic farewell to Stills**—a song about their **complicated relationship and the roads they had traveled together**.
- Stills later admitted he found the song **bittersweet**, as it seemed to **signal the end of their musical partnership**.

Even after their failed album, **Stills and Young couldn't stay away from each other for long**.

The Legacy of Stills and Young's Collaborations

CSNY – The Push-and-Pull Dynamic

Whenever **Crosby, Stills, Nash & Young** reunited, the Stills-Young rivalry **reignited**.

- Young would often **join and leave unpredictably**, frustrating Stills and Nash.

- Stills, as always, wanted **strong leadership** in the band, while Young preferred to **work on his own terms**.
- Their **onstage battles** became legendary, with both men **trying to outplay each other on guitar solos**.

Despite their **differences**, whenever they did **collaborate**, the results were **electrifying**.

The Guitar Battles

One of the **most thrilling aspects** of Stills and Young's relationship was their **guitar duels**.

- Both were **phenomenal guitarists** but had **contrasting styles**:
    - **Stills played with precision**, using **jazz and blues influences**.

- ○ **Young played with raw power**, favoring **distorted, feedback-heavy solos**.
- In **live shows**, their competing solos turned into **epic musical battles**, especially on songs like:
  - ○ **"Southern Man"**
  - ○ **"Down by the River"**
  - ○ **"Carry On"**

Fans **loved these showdowns**, as they showcased the **fiery chemistry between the two musicians**.A Rivalry That Defined an Era

The relationship between **Stephen Stills and Neil Young** was **never simple**.

- They **inspired each other** to create some of their **best music**.

- They **challenged each other**, refusing to let the other become complacent.
- They **fought, broke up, and reunited repeatedly**, always drawn back to their undeniable **musical connection**.

Even as **age and time softened their battles**, their legacy remains. Stills and Young were **both geniuses in their own right**, but together, they created something even **more powerful**—a **rivalry-turned-brotherhood that pushed the boundaries of rock music**.

As Stills once said about Young:

*"He drives me crazy, but I wouldn't be where I am without him."* And Young, in a rare moment of sentimentality, once admitted: *"Stephen? He's a hell of a musician. Maybe the best I ever played with."* Their story is one of **competition,**

respect, and the eternal struggle between two titans of rock music.

# CHAPTER 9: LEGACY AND INFLUENCE

Stephen Stills is often regarded as **one of the most versatile, innovative, and influential musicians of his generation**. Whether through **Buffalo Springfield, Crosby, Stills & Nash (and Young), Manassas, his solo career, or his collaborations with other legendary artists**, Stills shaped the sound of **folk rock, country rock, and blues rock** in ways that still resonate today.

This chapter explores how **Stills' music inspired future generations**, the **enduring power of his work**, and how his **contributions**

**to rock music continue to be celebrated through covers, tributes, and reinterpretations**.

How Stills Inspired Future Generations

The Birth of the Singer-Songwriter Movement

Stills was a **key figure in the rise of the singer-songwriter movement** of the 1970s. His ability to **blend poetic lyrics with intricate guitar work and rich vocal harmonies** influenced countless artists who came after him.

- His **introspective, personal songwriting** paved the way for artists like **Jackson Browne, James Taylor, and Bonnie Raitt**.
- The **confessional storytelling** in songs like **"Helplessly Hoping"** and **"4 + 20"**

set a blueprint for future singer-songwriters.

- His mix of **acoustic folk and electric blues guitar** became a defining characteristic of **'70s folk rock.**

Even artists from **later generations**, like **Dave Matthews, John Mayer, and Ryan Adams**, have cited **Stills' influence on their songwriting and guitar style.**

A Pioneer of Genre-Blending

One of Stills' greatest contributions was his **ability to seamlessly blend multiple musical genres.**

- In **Buffalo Springfield**, he combined **folk, rock, and psychedelia.**

- With **CSN(&Y)**, he helped create the **harmony-driven folk-rock sound**.
- **Manassas** fused **blues, country, rock, and Latin influences**—a style that predated the **alt-country and Americana movements**.
- His **solo work incorporated jazz, R&B, and even Caribbean rhythms**.

This willingness to **experiment and evolve** has influenced artists across genres, from **Wilco and My Morning Jacket** to **modern blues musicians like Gary Clark Jr.**.

Influence on Guitarists

Stills has long been recognized as **one of the most technically gifted guitarists in rock history**.

- **Eric Clapton** once praised his **versatility and skill**, calling him **"one of the best all-around players"** he had ever worked with.
- Stills' ability to **switch between acoustic fingerpicking, bluesy electric solos, and Latin-inspired rhythms** has influenced generations of guitarists.
- **His unique tunings and intricate picking style** can be heard in the work of **Lindsey Buckingham (Fleetwood Mac), Mark Knopfler (Dire Straits), and even Eddie Vedder (Pearl Jam)**.

Cover Versions and Tributes

Artists Who Have Covered Stills' Songs

Stills' **songwriting and musicianship** have inspired many artists to cover his songs, keeping his legacy alive. Some of the most notable covers include:

- **"Love the One You're With"** – Covered by **Luther Vandross, The Isley Brothers, and The Supremes**.
- **"For What It's Worth"** – Reinterpreted by **Public Enemy, Rush, and Kid Rock**.
- **"Helplessly Hoping"** – Performed by artists like **Alison Krauss & Union Station and Mumford & Sons**.
- **"Southern Cross"** – A favorite among **Jimmy Buffett and country artists**, demonstrating the song's enduring appeal.

Each of these covers **introduced Stills' music to new audiences**, ensuring that his influence would continue to grow across generations.

Tribute Albums and Recognition

Over the years, Stills has been honored with various **tributes and accolades**:

- **In 1997, he became the first artist inducted into the Rock & Roll Hall of Fame twice in one night** (for Buffalo Springfield and Crosby, Stills & Nash).
- **Grammy Lifetime Achievement Award** – Recognizing his contributions to rock music.
- **A series of tribute concerts and albums** featuring musicians like **Bruce Springsteen, Dave Matthews, and Sheryl Crow**.

These honors reflect **how deeply his music has resonated across generations**.

The Enduring Power of His Music

Even decades after his peak, **Stephen Stills' music continues to be relevant**.

- **His protest songs remain powerful**, especially in times of social unrest. **"For What It's Worth"** is still used in films, commercials, and political movements.
- **His love songs and introspective ballads** continue to touch people on a personal level. Songs like **"Suite: Judy Blue Eyes"** and **"4 + 20"** remain deeply moving.
- **His guitar work continues to be studied by new generations of musicians**, proving that his musical legacy is still alive.

As long as **people are searching for music with passion, intelligence, and soul, Stephen Stills' songs will never fade away**.

## A Legend Who Shaped Rock History

Stephen Stills is more than just a **great songwriter and musician**—he is a **foundational figure in rock history**.

- He helped define **the sound of the 1960s and 1970s**.
- He pioneered **genre fusion** before it was even recognized as a movement.
- His music remains **as vital and influential today as it was decades ago**.

Whether through **his groundbreaking work with Buffalo Springfield, his timeless contributions to CSN(&Y), his fearless solo career, or his continued dedication to making music**, Stills' **impact on rock and folk music is undeniable**.

As fans, musicians, and historians continue to **rediscover his work**, one thing remains clear:

**Stephen Stills' music will always be a part of the soundtrack of our lives.**

# CONCLUSION

The Lasting Legacy of Stephen Stills

Few artists have left as deep an imprint on **rock, folk, and blues music** as **Stephen Stills**. From his early days as a **folk guitarist in Greenwich Village** to his rise with **Buffalo Springfield**, his superstardom with **Crosby, Stills & Nash (and Young)**, and his ambitious solo projects, Stills has always been a musician who **pushed boundaries and defied expectations**.

His songs are more than just **melodies and lyrics**—they are **snapshots of history**, reflections of love, loss, and revolution. His guitar playing isn't just skilled—it's **groundbreaking, blending genres in ways that few have ever mastered**. His voice carries the

**raw emotion of someone who has lived the music he writes**.

A Trailblazer in Sound and Spirit

Stills was never content to stay in one place musically. He was a:

- **Folk purist when the scene demanded authenticity**
- **Psychedelic explorer when the '60s called for revolution**
- **Blues-rock virtuoso when guitar-driven music took center stage**
- **Latin and jazz experimenter when the industry stayed stuck in formulas**

He didn't follow trends—he created them. His **genre-blending style** inspired countless artists, and his **refusal to compromise** set a standard for artistic integrity.

A Legacy That Lives On

Even as new generations of musicians emerge, **Stills' influence remains undeniable**.

- **His songs continue to be covered and rediscovered** by artists across genres.
- **His guitar work is still studied** by musicians who want to learn from a true master.
- **His messages of love, social awareness, and personal introspection still resonate today**.

Many artists fade with time, but Stills' music still **feels as fresh, relevant, and powerful** as when it was first recorded. His ability to write songs that speak to **the heart and the mind**, that blend **technical brilliance with raw emotion**, is why his work **stands the test of time**.

The Man Behind the Music

Stephen Stills has always been a **deeply passionate and complex artist**.

- He is **known for his intensity**, sometimes clashing with bandmates, but always driven by a pursuit of musical excellence.
- He has **faced personal struggles** but never let them silence his voice.
- He has **lived through the highest highs and lowest lows** of the music industry, yet he never stopped playing, writing, and evolving.

He is, at his core, an artist who **lives for music**—not for fame, not for money, but for the love of the craft.

Final Thoughts: The Soundtrack of a Lifetime

Stephen Stills once said:

*"Music is a living thing. It has to keep growing, changing, and moving, or it dies."*

That philosophy is why his music **still matters today**. It is why his songs continue to **inspire, comfort, and challenge** listeners around the world. His legacy is more than just **awards and accolades**—it is the **soundtrack to countless lives**, the **melodies that define moments**, and the **lyrics that tell stories of an era that shaped the world**.

As long as people **pick up guitars, harmonize in three-part vocals, and search for meaning through music**, Stephen Stills' work will continue to **live on and inspire**.

His music is timeless.

His legacy is eternal.

**Stephen Stills: The Soundtrack of the '60s and '70s – The Stories Behind the Songs** is more than just a book title. It is a statement of fact.

Because **his music was, is, and always will be the soundtrack of a generation—and beyond.**

THE END

Made in United States
North Haven, CT
07 August 2025

71448002R00085